First Sonatina Albu
by James and Jane Smisor Bastien

Contents

ISBN 0-8497-5242-6
© 1984 Kjos West, 4382 Jutland Drive, San Diego, California.
International copyright secured. Printed in U.S.A.

WP124

To the student

First Sonatina Album provides representative literature at the early intermediate level. Themes are identified in this edition to assist learning the sonatina form.

Most sonatinas serve as models to study before playing more difficult sonatas later. In this regard, a sonatina is a little sonata.

Practice Suggestions

1. Practice hands *separately* to establish the basic hand motions.
2. Practice in *sections*.
3. Practice *slowly* at first; keep a steady beat; and gradually increase the tempo. A metronome may be used to help control the tempo.

Memory Suggestions

1. Analyze the form of each movement.
2. Learn each section of each movement from memory; be able to start at any section from memory.
3. Know the tonality (key) in each section of each movement. Analyze the harmony used in each movement.

Contest Reminders

Sonatinas are often used in auditions and contests. The examiner or judge will be observing these points:

- correct notes and rhythm
- steady tempo
- correct dynamics and phrasing (touch)
- correct balance of melody and accompaniment
- appropriate style and mood of each movement necessary for a convincing performance

Sonatina in C
by William Duncombe

William Duncombe, a late eighteenth century English composer, came from a musical family. For generations the Duncombes were one of the leading musical and literary families in England. In 1785 he published two volumes titled *Progressive Lessons for the Harpsichord and Piano Forte* which contained his best-known compositions.

Sonatina in G
by Thomas Attwood

Thomas Attwood (1765-1838), an English organist and composer, studied with Mozart. In 1796 he became the organist at St. Paul's Cathedral in London. He was a close friend of Mendelssohn, who dedicated some organ works to Attwood.

Allegretto

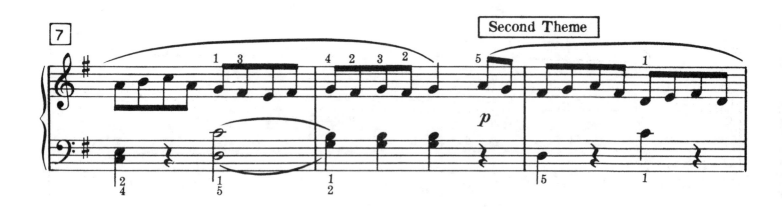

II.

Andante

First Theme

III. Rondo

Vivace

Sonatina in Romantic Style
by James Bastien

I.

Allegro moderato (♩=100)

WP124

Closing Theme

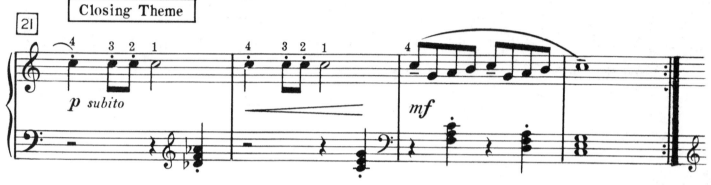

DEVELOPMENT
Second Theme

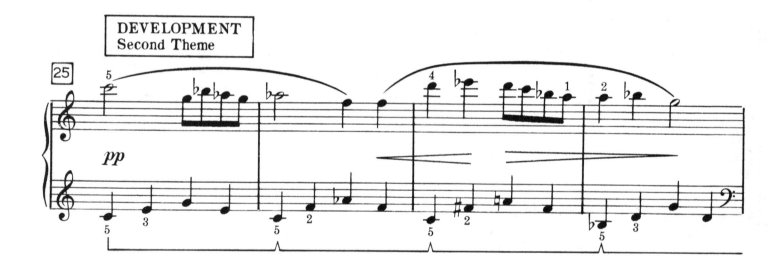

RECAPITULATION
Second Theme

Closing Theme

II. Interlude

Andante

III. Rondo

Sonatina in C
by Tobias Haslinger

Tobias Haslinger (1787-1842), was best known as a German music publisher, although he did write some piano compositions. He was a friend of Beethoven.

I.

First Theme

Coda

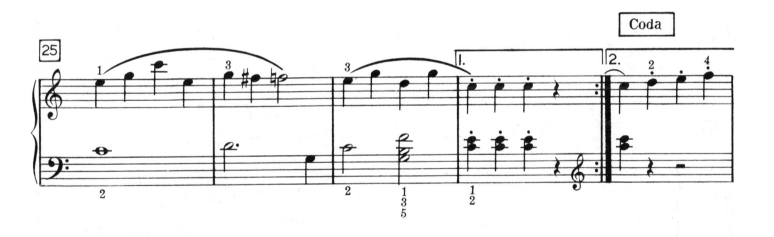

II.

Allegretto

First Theme

Coda

Sonatina in F
by Ludwig van Beethoven

I.

II. Rondo

*This rolled chord can be played more easily by students in this manner:

First Theme

Third Theme